Introduction

All animals have babies, some start out in an egg while others are carried in a pouch or in the mother's tummy until it is time to be born.

Let's start with a fun fact, baby monkeys will make babbling noises like a human baby until they can learn to communicate.

 **is for an Antling.**

An antling is a baby ant.

Ants start off as tiny eggs which the queen lays in the ant hill.

It takes ants 6 - 10 weeks to grow to be an adult.

My First Book about the Alphabet of Baby Animals

Amazing Animal Books Children's Picture Books

By Molly Davidson

Mendon Cottage Books

JD-Biz Publishing

Read More Amazing Animal Books

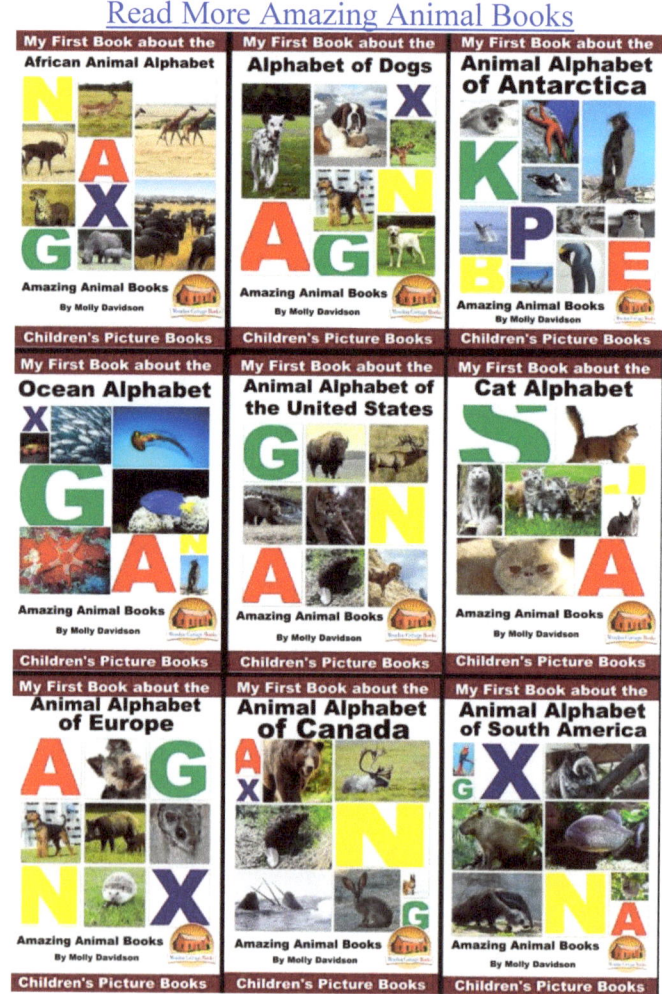

Purchase at Amazon.com

Download Free Books!
http://MendonCottageBooks.com

 **is for a Baby.**

Many animals like apes, humans, and lemurs call their babies, a baby.

Baby apes stay in their mothers for about 8 months until they are born.

Lemurs take 4 1/2 - 5 1/2 months to be born.

B is also for a Bunny.

Baby rabbits are called bunnies, but some people just call all rabbits bunnies, but it really only means the baby ones.

Bunnies only take about one month to be born.

 **is for a Calf.**

Calf is a very common name for a baby animal; most mammal babies are called calves.

Animals that have baby calves are antelope, whales, cows, elephants, giraffes, moose, camels, dolphins, rhinos, and the list goes on.

C is also for a Chick.

Most birds, including penguins, emus, chickens, hummingbirds, falcons, etc, call their babies a chick.

Chickens must lay their eggs then sit on them to keep them warm for 21 days until they hatch.

Lastly, C also stands for Cubs.

Cubs are baby bears, hyenas, walruses, and raccoons.

Polar bears are born in just 2 months, but brown bears take 7 1/2 months to be born.

D is for a Duckling.

Ducklings are baby ducks.

Just like a chicken, ducks have to lay their eggs and sit on them for 28 days until they hatch.

 **is for an Eaglet.**

An eaglet is a baby eagle.

Eagles usually lay two eggs in a nest made of sticks, mud, and leaves.

The babies hatch out of the eggs at around 35 days.

 **is for Fawn.**

A baby deer or antelope is known as a fawn.

Deer take 6 1/2 months to have their babies, usually two at a time.

Most fawns are born with white spots and many loose them as they grow to be an adult.

F

is also for a Flapper.

Flappers are what baby swans are called.

After the swan has laid her eggs, the flappers will hatch in about 6 weeks.

Babies are born with soft downy grey feathers, which they loose and get smooth white ones.

G is for a Gosling.

A gosling is a baby goose.

Goslings take 4 - 5 weeks to hatch, and may take up to 3 days to break through their egg's shell.

H is for a Hatchling.

Hatchlings are baby alligators, crocodiles, dinosaurs, and turtles.

Alligators will lay 35 - 90 eggs in a nest covered with weeds for warmth.

Hatchlings take about 2 months to hatch.

I is for an Infant.

Most primates, which are monkeys, baboons, and gorillas, called their babies an infant.

Most primates carry their babies inside themselves for 6 months until they are born.

Monkeys are usually born a different color than their parents, then they change at 6 months.

 is for a Joey.

A baby kangaroo, koala, opossum, and wombat are all known as a joey.

K is for a Kitten.

Most baby cats, including wild cats like the bobcat, cheetah, and mountain lion, are called kittens.

Pet cats take about 2 months to give birth, but many wild cats take over 3 months.

K is also for a Kit.

Foxes, skunks, muskrats, and woodchucks called their babies kits.

Fox take about 7 weeks to give birth, skunks are about 9 weeks, and woodchucks are only 4 weeks.

L is for Larva.

Before most insects, including bees, gnats, wasps, and termites, become adults they start out as larva, which is like little worm.

L is for a Lamb.

A baby sheep is called a lamb and they are usually born as a twin after 5 months.

 **is for a Maggot.**

Baby flies are called maggots, which is like a worm that will one day turn into a fly.

Fly eggs hatch in less than 24 hours, and then stay a maggot for only 3 - 5 days before becoming an adult flying fly.

 **is for a Nymph.**

Nymph is used to describe the babies of most flying insects like grasshoppers, beetles, mosquitoes, and lice.

Some nymphs can breathe underwater.

 **is for an Owlet.**

An owlet is the name given to a baby owl, which after being laid hatches in about one month.

P is for a Pup.

Some animals that call their babies pups are bats, coyotes, mice, dogs, wolves, seals, sharks, rats, prairie dogs, moles, etc.

 **is for Shoat.**

Baby pigs, boars, and hogs are called shoats or piglets.

Shoats take about 4 months to be born.

In the first 2 weeks they can recognize their mother's voice and will come running to her.

T is for a Tadpole.

Before frogs and toads turn into an adult they start out as a tadpole.

Frogs take 3 - 25 days to hatch into a tadpole, the warmer the water the faster they will hatch.

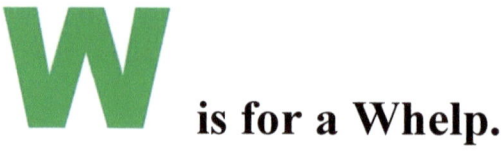 **is for a Whelp.**

Baby otters and tigers are called whelps.

Otters are born in 2 months and are about the same length as their mother!

Whelp tigers take 3 - 4 months to be born.

 **is for Yearlings.**

New baby horses are called colts if they are a boy or fillies if they are a girl, but when they turn one they get another title, which is a yearling.

Conclusion

I hope you have enjoyed reading about many amazing baby animals.

One more fact, baby elephants take almost 2 years to be born, which is the longest of any animal.

Download Free Books!

http://MendonCottageBooks.com

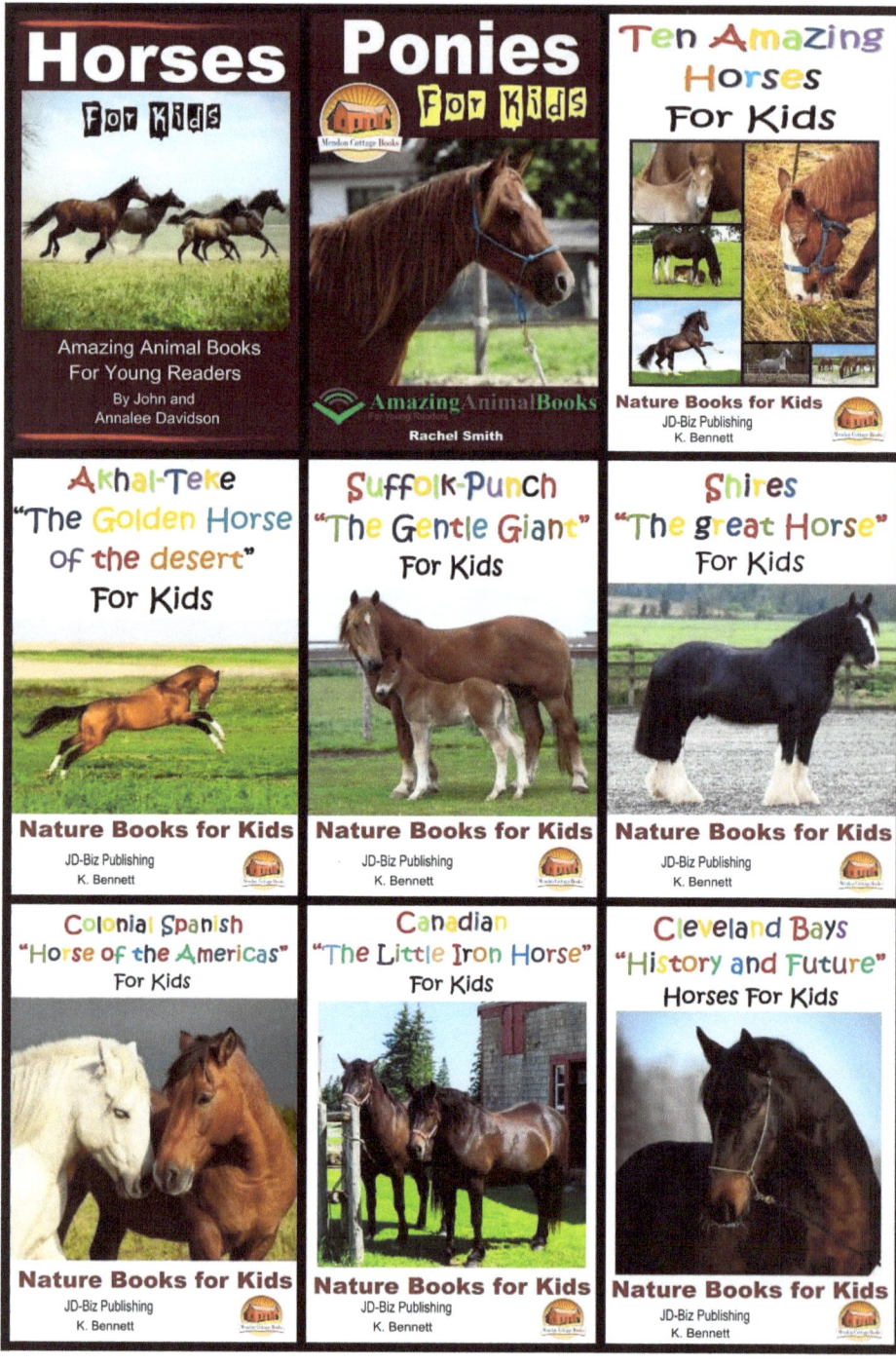

Our books are available at

1. Amazon.com

2. Barnes and Noble

3. Itunes

4. Kobo

5. Smashwords

6. Google Play Books

Download Free Books!
http://MendonCottageBooks.com

Publisher

JD-Biz Corp

P O Box 374

Mendon, Utah 84325

http://www.jd-biz.com/